Where is it?
Is it moving?

• • • • • • • • • • • • • • • •

Contents

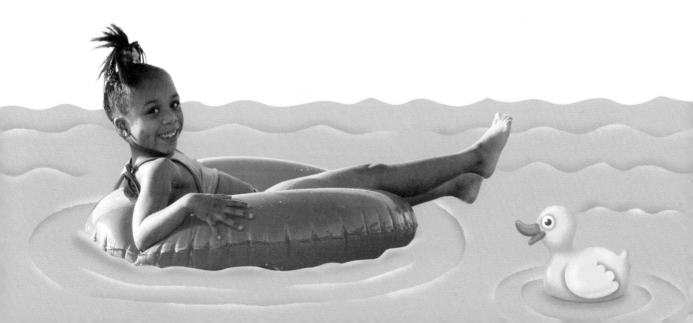

Where is it?

A bird
is in the
birdbath.

A bird
is out of the
birdbath.

A dog
jumps over
the fence.

A dog
digs under
the fence.

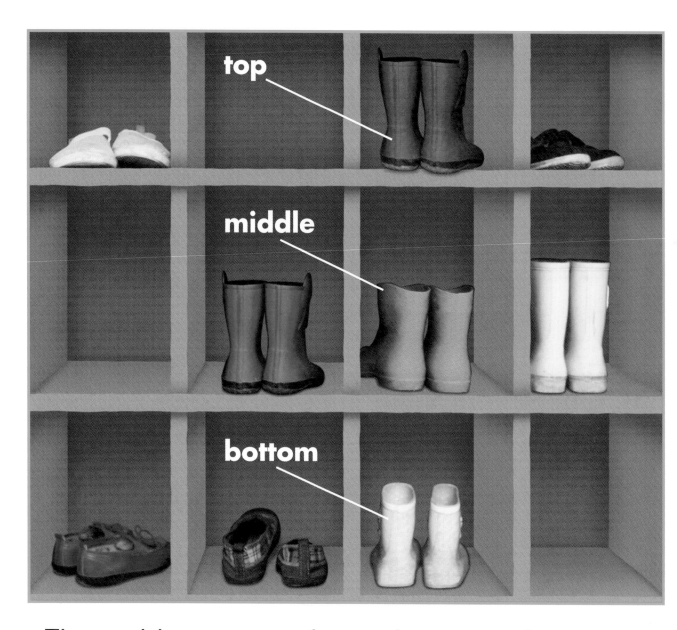

The red boots are above the green boots.

The yellow boots are below the green boots.

A cat is
in front of
the cat bed.

A cat is
in back of
the cat bed.

 A fork is to the left of the plate.

A spoon is to the right of the plate.

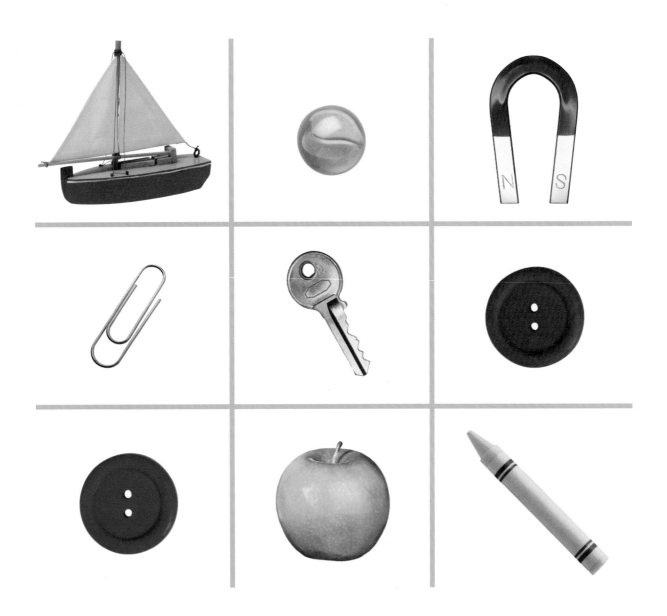

We can tell where something is.

We can tell the **position** of something.

What is the position of the red button?

Is it moving?

Some things move fast.

Some things move slowly.

9

Some things roll.

Some things slide.

Some things move in a circle.

Some things move in a straight line.

Why is it moving?

We can push things. A push is a **force**.

We can pull things. A pull is a force.

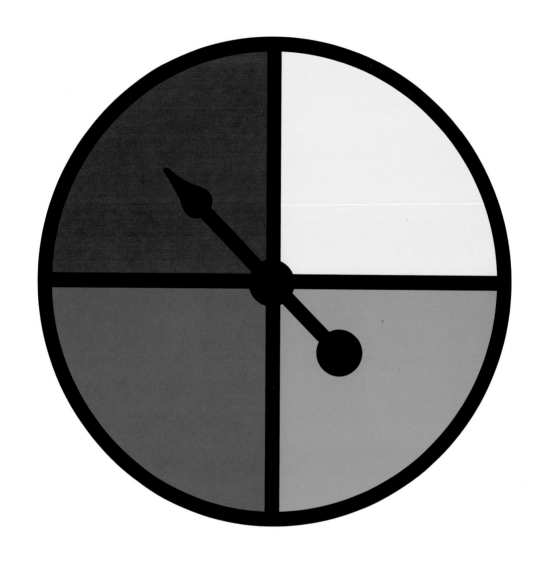

How can we change the **direction**?

A force can change the direction.

How can we change the **speed**?

A force can change the speed.

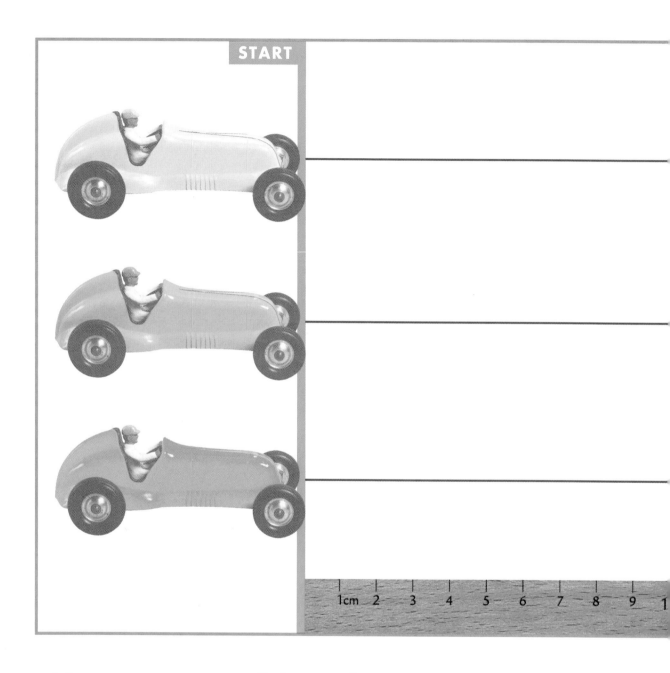

START

1cm 2 3 4 5 6 7 8 9 1

How can we tell how far an object moves?

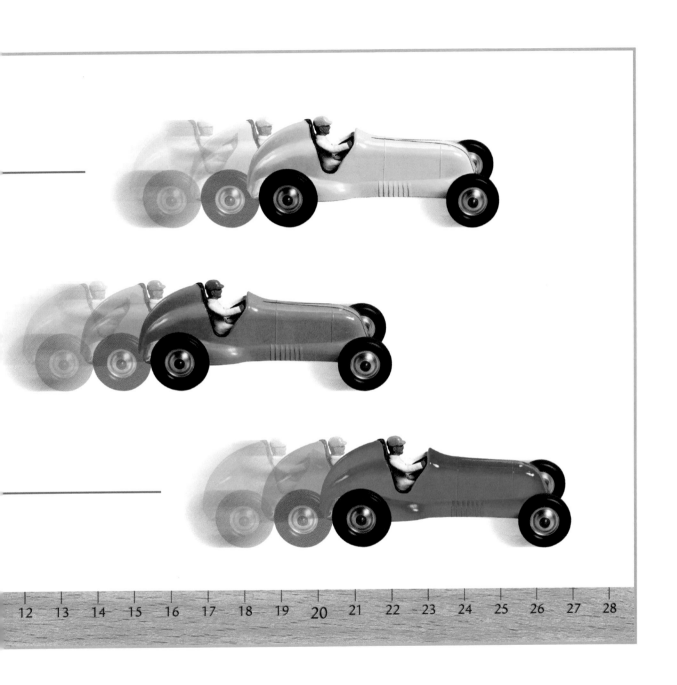

We can **measure**.

Glossary

direction the way an object faces

force a push or a pull

measure to find out how far something has moved

position where something is

speed how fast or slowly something moves